Come and Praise 2

Compiled by Geoffrey Marshall-Taylor
Arrangements by Douglas Coombes

BBC ACTIVE

To order any BBC Active resources for schools,
call 0845 313 9999 (Monday–Friday, 8.30am–5.30pm),
order online at **www.pearsonschools.co.uk/bbcactive**,
or write to: BBC Active Customer Services, PO Box 88,
Harlow, Essex CM20 2JE. Fax: 0845 313 7777
Visit the BBC Schools website to find great online resources:
www.bbc.co.uk/schools

BBC Active, an imprint of Educational Publishers LLP,
Edinburgh Gate, Harlow, Essex, CM20 2JE, England.

ISBN 978-0-563-34247-2

Printed in Malaysia (CTP-VVP)

This anthology is a sequel to the 72 songs in *Come and Praise 1*. For this reason the numbering of items in this book begins at 73.

Acknowledgement is due to the following, whose permission is required for reproduction of the words of the hymns:

73: Words: (c) Anne Conlon. Commissioned for BBC Songs of Praise by WWFUK; *74:* words Copyright Ann Sutcliffe; *75:* words reproduced by permission of Stainer & Bell Ltd; *76:* words reproduced by permission of Stainer & Bell Ltd; *77:* words by Geoffrey Gardner; *78:* words by David Self, reprinted with his permission; *79:* words by Geoffrey Gardner; *80:* words by Simon Fitter, used with his permission; *81:* words (c) Arthur Scholey; *82:* words reproduced by permission of Stainer & Bell Ltd; *83* and *85:* words by Geoffrey Gardner; *86:*words reproduced by permission of Stainer & Bell Ltd; *87:* words by Geoffrey Gardner; *88:* words (c) Arthur Scholey; *89:* words by David Stoll; *90:* words reproduced by permission of Stainer & Bell Ltd; *91:* words by Geoffrey Gardner; *92:* words by Geoffrey Gardner; *93:* words by Jill Darby, printed by permission of BTW Music; *96:* Copyright words by Jancis Harvey; *98:* words by Stuart Dauermann and Steffi Geiser Rubin, (c) 1975 Lillenas Publishing Company. All rights reserved. Used by permission; *99:* words (c) 1985 Patrick Appleford; *100:* words by Ronald H. Green. Copyright Kevin Mayhew Ltd. Used by permission from Hymns Old and New, Licence No. 884082; *101:* words by Geoffrey Gardner; *102:* words used by permission of Salvationist Publishing & Supplies Ltd; *103:* Copyright words Jancis Harvey; *104:* words reproduced by permission of Stainer & Bell Ltd; *105:* extra words by Geoffrey Gardner; *106:* words by Geoffrey Gardner; *109:* words by Susan Sayers. Copyright by Kevin Mayhew Ltd. Used with permission from Hymns Old and New, Licence No. 884081; *111:* words by Geoffrey Gardner; *112:* words by Alison Carver; *113:* (To everything there is a season) Words from the Book of Ecclesiastes. Adaptation by Peter Seeger. (c) 1962 Melody Trails Inc. Assigned to TRO Essex Music Ltd; *114:* words by Geoffrey Gardner; *115:* words (c) Arthur Scholey on behalf of Albert House Press; *117:* words by Elizabeth Bennett; *118:* words (c) Arthur Scholey; *120:* words by Cecily Taylor; *122:* words by Geoffrey Gardner; *124:* words by Pete Ratcliffe, (c) Pete Ratcliffe/Jubilate Hymns; *125:* words by Sydney Carter, (c) 1963 TRO Essex Music Ltd, 19–20 Poland Street, London W1V 3DD. International Copyright secured. All rights reserved. Used by permission; *126:* Copyright words Jancis Harvey; *127:* words by Geoffrey Gardner; *128:* words reproduced by permission of Stainer & Bell Ltd; *129:* words reproduced by permission of Stainer & Bell Ltd; *131:* words by J M C Crum, printed by permission of Oxford University Press; *132:* words by Alan Dale, printed by permission of Oxford University Press; *133:* Copyright words Jancis Harvey; *134:* words (c) Arthur Scholey; *135:* words by Rev Paul Booth with his permission to change the words as required; *136:* words by Robert Smith; *137:* words (c) Estelle White 1984. Used with permission; *138:* words by Alex Mitchell, with permission from Leadership Today; *139:* words (c) Arthur Scholey; *140:* words adapted from Sanskrit by Satish Kumar; *141:* words adapted by Geoffrey Gardner; *145:* words by Roger Courtney (c) Roger Courtney; *146:* words reproduced by permission of Stainer & Bell Ltd; *147:* words by Sebastian Temple. Copyright Franciscan Communications, USA; *148:* words by Geoffrey Gardner.

Contents

Continued overleaf

HARVEST

PEACE

73

1 When your Father made the world, before that
world was old,
In his eye what he had made was lovely to
behold.
Help your people to care for your world.

Chorus:
The world is a garden you made,
And you are the one who planted the seed,
The world is a garden you made,
A life for our food, life for our joy,
Life we could kill with our selfish greed.

2 And the world that he had made, the seas, the
rocks, the air,
All the creatures and the plants he gave into
our care.
Help your people to care for your world.
Chorus

3 When you walked in Galilee, you said your
Father knows
When each tiny sparrow dies, each fragile lily
grows.
Help your people to care for your world.
Chorus

4 And the children of the earth, like sheep
within your fold,
Should have food enough to eat, and shelter
from the cold.
Help your people to care for your world.
Chorus

Ann Conlon

This was written for the World Wide Fund for
Nature.

74

1 Sad, puzzled eyes of small, hungry children,
Thin, weary bodies tending the ground;
Weak, pleading voices begging in cities;
They long for the day when food is shared
round.

Chorus:
Prayers of sorrow, prayers of loving,
Looking for ways to give and to share.
Learning, explaining, helping, supporting;
Show all the world how deeply we care.

2 Rumbling earthquakes, villages topple;
Drought shrivels cattle, harvests and men,
Flood waters swirling, drowning and surging,
Despairing survivors begin life again.
Chorus

3 Terror and death in war shattered countries,
Misery, tears, deep longing for peace.
Refugees flee — no hope for the future;
How long must they wait for suffering to
cease?
Chorus

Ann Sutcliffe

75

1 I saw the man from Galilee
Who told a message new.
The hungry crowd had gathered round,
To see what he could do.
And in his words was hope;
And in his hands was bread.
'Come, share this bread,
And share my life —
My life for you,' he said.

8

2 I saw a boy with barley loaves;
  He had some small fish too.
  'I can't do much, but I can share:
  Lord Jesus, it's for you.
  For in your words is hope
  And in your hands is bread.
  I'll share my bread,
  And know your love —
  Your life for me,' he said.

3 I saw a rich young man, who came
  To speak to Jesus too.
  'I want to live, I don't know how,'
  He said, 'What can I do?'
  And Jesus answered, 'This
  Is life, to share your bread.
  Sell all you have,
  Give to the poor,
  Life can be yours,' he said.

4 I saw the whole world in the eyes
  Of one small hungry boy.
  There is no hope, there is no life,
  There is no sign of joy.
  And how can there be hope,
  Where people have no bread?
  They struggle on,
  And try to live,
  But life hangs by a thread.
      Yet Jesus shows us hope,
      For in his hands is bread;
      Bread for the world,
      If all will share:
      He is the living bread.

George A. Chalmers

76

1 God in his love for us lent us this planet.
  Gave it a purpose in time and in space:
  Small as a spark from the fire of creation,
  Cradle of life and the home of our race.

2 Thanks be to God for its bounty and beauty,
  Life that sustains us in body and mind:
  Plenty for all, if we learn how to share it,
  Riches undreamed of to fathom and find.

3 Long have the wars of man ruined its harvest:
  Long has earth bowed to the terror of force:
  Long have we wasted what others have need
  of,
  Poisoned the fountain of life at its source.

4 Earth is the Lord's: it is ours to enjoy it.
  Ours, as his stewards, to farm and defend.
  From its pollution, misuse, and destruction.
  Good Lord, deliver us, world without end!

Fred Pratt Green

77

1 The sun burns hot and dry
  High in the cloudless sky,
  No shade.
  The soil is crumbling dust,
  Like powder at the touch.

2 The brittle corn is crushed,
  Away blow empty husks,
  No food.
  No life left in the grain,
  The seed has failed again.

3 Empty hands, reaching out,
  But there's nothing there.
  Cracking lips,
  Withered skin,
  The eyes just stare.

4 The cows and goats are thin,
 The bones show through the skin,
 No milk.
 They search for grass to graze,
 They swelter in the haze.

5 The wells are empty holes,
 The river only stones,
 No drink.
 When will a storm cloud burst
 To satisfy the thirst?

6 Then it came, cooling rain,
 Falling all around;
 Everywhere,
 Muddy pools, form in the ground.

7 The desert dances on,
 Now water has come down,
 New life.
 And seeds of hope begin.
 How long will be the spring?
 How long will be the spring?

Geoffrey Gardner

78 1 By brother sun who brings the day,
 And sheds his dazzling light,
 And warms the world with welcome ray;
 By sister moon and sister stars,
 Who turn throughout the night,
 Above in heaven as they shine:
 Be praised by all your creatures, Lord,
 To you all praise belongs!

2 By brother wind and brother air
   On cloudy days and bright,
   In weather stormy, calm or fair;
   By sister water, precious pure,
   Whose taste is cool delight —
   Most humble yet reviving drink:
   Be praised by all your creatures, Lord,
   To you all praise belongs!

3 By brother fire, robust and strong,
   Who gives us heat and might,
   With you now join we all our song,
   And with our sister earth as well,
   With whom we all unite
   To sing with flowers, fruit and grass:
   Be praised by all your creatures, Lord,
   To you all praise belongs!

David Self

This is based on a poem by St Francis of Assisi.

79

1 (1) From the tiny ant,
  (2) *From the tiny ant,*
  (1) To the elephant,
  (2) *To the elephant,*
  (1) From the snake to the kangaroo,
  (2) *From the snake to the kangaroo,*
  (1) From the great white shark,
  (2) *From the great white shark,*
  (1) To the singing lark,
  (2) *To the singing lark,*
  (1) Care for them, it's up to you
  (2) *Care for them, it's up to you,*
  (1 & 2) Care for them it's up to you,
  (1 & 2) Care for them it's up to you.
  (1 & 2) No one else will care for them,
  (1) It's up
  (2) *It's up*
  (1 & 2) It's up to you.

2 (1) From the tabby cat,
  (2) *From the tabby cat,*
  (1) To the desert rat,
  (2) *To the desert rat,*
  (1) From the hamster to the chimpanzee,
  (2) *From the hamster to the chimpanzee,*
  (1) From the common tern,
  (2) *From the common tern,*
  (1) To the crawling worm,
  (2) *To the crawling worm,*
  (1) Care for them, it's up to me,
  (2) *Care for them, it's up to me,*
  (1 & 2) Care for them it's up to me,
  (1 & 2) Care for them it's up to me.
  (1 & 2) No one else will care for them,
  (1) It's up
  (2) *It's up*
  (1 & 2) It's up to me.

3 (1) From the mongrel dog,
  (2) *From the mongrel dog,*
  (1) To the snorting hog,
  (2) *To the snorting hog,*
  (1) From the badger to the platypus,
  (2) *From the badger to the platypus,*
  (1) From the small minnow,
  (2) *From the small minnow,*
  (1) To the white rhino,
  (2) *To the white rhino,*
  (1) Care for them it's up to us,
  (2) *Care for them it's up to us,*
  (1 & 2) Care for them it's up to us,
  (1 & 2) Care for them it's up to us.
  (1 & 2) No one else will care for them,
  (1) It's up
  (2) *It's up*
  (1 & 2) It's up to us.

Geoffrey Gardner

*This song can be sung by two groups, indicated by
(1) and (2). Generally, group (2) echoes group
(1). If you prefer, everyone can sing every line.*

80

1 All the animals that I have ever seen,
Big ones, little ones, and others in between,
Four legs, two legs,
Some no legs at all;
I like them all.

2 All the animals that like your strokes and pats,
Dogs and hamsters, gerbils, guinea pigs and
cats,
Mice and tortoises,
Rabbits in the hutch;
I like so much.

3 All the animals that fly up in the sky,
Robins, wrens, and butterflies that flutter by,
Magpies, dragonflies,
And the bumble bee;
I like to see.

4 All the animals I only see at night,
Hedgehog, nightingale and owl with eyes so
bright.
Fox and badger,
Moths and bat and shrew;
I like them too.

5 All the animals that live beneath the sea,
Shrimps and prawns and jellyfish that tickle
me,
Starfish, anemones,
Crabs beneath my feet!
I like to meet.

6 There are animals I'll never see at all,
Some live overseas, and some are just too
small,
All God's animals,
Need the care we give,
If they're to live.

Simon Fitter

81

1 What about being old Moses
And slogging across the sand,
Escaping through the wilderness
To reach the Promised Land?

To be old Moses would be a mistake;
Today the fun of it is
That we've only one world and we can make
Our Promised Land from this!

2 What about being Saint Brendon,
For mile after nautical mile,
He plunged across fantastic seas
In search of the Blessed Isle?

To be Saint Brendon would be a mistake;
Today the fun of it is
That we've only one world and we can make
Our blessed isle from this!

3 What about being Columbus
And seeking another way round,
With oceans still to voyage on,
And more new worlds to be found?

To be Columbus would be a mistake;
Today the fun of it is
That we've only one world and we can make
Our new world out of this!

4 What about taking a space-ship
And flying to space unknown.
There must be worlds enough to give
Us each one of his own?

To take a space-ship would be a mistake;
Today the fun of it is
That we've only one world and we can make
Our one world out of this!

Arthur Scholey

St Brendon (484–577 A.D.) was an Irish Christian who sailed for several years to find 'paradise amid the waves'. Christopher Columbus (1451–1506) was an Italian explorer.

82

1 It's the springs up in the mountains make the
rivers of the plain,
That bring water to the cities as they seek the
sea again,
And the rivers fill the oceans and the oceans
make the rain.
By the winds blowing over one world.

Chorus:
And a man becomes a neighbour or a brother
or a friend,
When the one-ness of the world you understand.
And the east for your neighbour is another
neighbour's west.
It depends upon just where you stand.

2 There are people in the mountains and the
valleys down below,
There are people in the tropics, there are
people in the snow,
Some are happy, some are homeless folk who
have no place to go,
But we all have to live in one world.
Chorus

3 There are workers for their wages out in field
and factory,
There are fishers for our food supply in boats
upon the sea;
There are people still imprisoned in the cage of
poverty,
As we labour for life in one world.
Chorus

4 As the sun lights up the morning, and another
day is found,
It's a gift to all that's living, that the world still
spins around,
And the night is still the day but seen the other
way around,
As the sun shines upon this one world.
Chorus

Richard Tysoe

83

Chorus:
I'm going to paint a perfect picture,
A world of make believe;
No more hunger, war or suffering,
The world I'd like to see.

1 The blackbird sings in the hedgerow,
The white owl sleeps in the barn,
The brown geese fly, a group in the sky,
The yellow chick pecks the corn.
Chorus

2 The stream runs clear through the meadow,
The wheat ears swell with the grain,
The oak trees give them shelter and shade,
The sunlight bursts through the rain.
Chorus

3 The farmers gather the harvest,
The children play by the mill,
The cattle chew and flick up their tails,
The ponies graze on the hill.

Chorus
I'm going to paint a perfect picture,
A world of make believe;
No more hunger, war or suffering,
The world I'd like to see,
The world I'd like to see.

Geoffrey Gardner

*This song describes a world where all races (verse
1), all the world's resources (verse 2) and all the
world's creatures (verse 3) are in perfect
harmony.*

84

1 Waves are beating on the shore,
  Crashing into foam,
  Seagulls squealing, wheeling high,
  Sailors coming home.
  Boats are bobbing up and down,
  Safe in harbour now,
  Some are riding out the storm,
  Dipping bow on bow.

2 God has made the sea so vast,
  Ocean's roaring swell;
  Cliffs of chalk and granite rocks,
  Sailors know them well;
  Furl the sails and winch the sheets,
  Feel the salt spray fly,
  Know the freedom of the sea,
  Underneath the sky.

3 Ever since the world began,
  People sailed the seas,
  Plunged across the roaring tides,
  Floated on the breeze;
  Feel the decks beneath your feet,
  See the golden sand,
  Set your feet upon the shore,
  Coming home to land.

Copyright controlled

85

1 Spirit of peace, come to our waiting world;
  Throughout the nations, may your voice be
  heard.
  Unlock the door of hope, for you hold the key
  Spirit of peace, come to our world.

2 Spirit of love, come to our waiting world;
  Throughout the nations, may your voice be
  heard.
  Unlock the door of hope, for you hold the key:
  Spirit of love, come to our world.

3 Spirit of strength, come to our waiting world;
Throughout the nations, may your voice be
heard.
Unlock the door of hope, for you hold the key;
Spirit of strength, come to our world.

4 Spirit of light, come to our waiting world;
Throughout the nations, may your voice be
heard.
Unlock the door of hope, for you hold the key;
Spirit of light, come to our world.

5 Spirit of God, come to our waiting world;
Throughout the nations, may your voice be
heard.
Unlock the door of hope, for you hold the key;
Spirit of God, come to our world.
Spirit of God, come to our world.

Geoffrey Gardner

1 The bell of creation is swinging for ever,
In all of the things that are coming to be,
The bell of creation is swinging for ever,
And all of the while it is swinging in me.

Chorus:
Swing, bell, over the land!
Swing, bell, under the sea!
The bell of creation is swinging for ever,
And all of the while it is swinging in me.

2 In all of my loving, in all of my labour
In all of the things that are coming to be,
In all of my loving, in all of my labour,
The bell of creation is swinging in me.

Chorus

3 I look to the life that is living for ever
In all of the things that are coming to be,
I look to the life that is living for ever
And all of the while it is looking for me.
Chorus

4 I'll swing with the bell that is swinging for ever,
In all of the things that are coming to be,
I'll swing with the bell that is swinging for ever,
And all of the while it is swinging in me.
Chorus

Sydney Carter

1 Give us hope, Lord, for each day,
Give us hope, Lord, for each day,
Guide our footsteps on the way,
Give us hope, Lord, for each day.

2 Give us strength, Lord, for each day . . .

3 Give us peace, Lord, for each day . . .

4 Give us love, Lord, for each day . . .

5 Give us joy, Lord, for each day . . .

Alternative words

1 Give us friends, Lord, for each day,
Give us friends, Lord, for each day,
Make us thankful on the way,
Give us friends, Lord, for each day.

2 Give us food, Lord, for each day . . .

3 Give us homes, Lord, for each day . . .

4 Give us clothes, Lord, for each day . . .

Geoffrey Gardner

The words by Geoffrey Gardner appear with the agreement of David Lynch, the composer of the music. David Lynch has requested that his original words, known as 'The Bell Song', be printed in addition.

The Bell Song

1 You gotta have love in your heart;
  You gotta have love in your heart;
  You knew it was Jesus right from the start;
  You gotta have love in your heart.

2 You gotta have peace on your mind;
  You gotta have peace on your mind;
  You knew it was Jesus there all the time;
  You gotta have peace on your mind.

3 You gotta have joy in your soul;
  You gotta have joy in your soul;
  The love of Jesus will make you whole;
  You gotta have peace in your soul.

                    David Lynch

1 I was lying in the roadway,
  Beaten, robbed and left to die,
  When someone passed the other side —
  I tried to catch his eye;
  But he kept staring straight ahead
  And quickly scurried by.
    Was that you, my friend,
    Was that you?
    Was that you, my friend,
    Was that you?
    Oh, I really was in need —
    Was that you?
    Was that you?

2 I was crying in the roadway,
Freezing cold and gripped in pain,
Then someone came across to see —
I dared to hope again;
But he just looked and hurried on
And left me in the rain.
Was that you, my friend,
Was that you?
Was that you, my friend,
Was that you?
Oh, I really was in need —
Was that you?
Was that you?

3 I was dying in the roadway,
And at last I knew despair,
For now, I saw with fading eyes,
My enemy stood there
But then he knelt, and lifted me,
And brought me safely here.
That was you, my friend,
That was you!
That was you, my friend,
That was you!
Oh, you were a friend in deed —
That was you!
That was you!

Arthur Scholey

A song based on the parable of the Good Samaritan (Luke 10.)

89

1 Guess how I feel,
  Sometimes,
  Nothing is real
  Sometimes,
  Everyone's living in dreams.
  Know what I think
  Sometimes,
  I've lost the link
  Sometimes,
  Nothing makes sense, so it seems:
  We've all become strange machines.
  But then I

  Chorus
  Look in the sky,
  Tell all the clouds to pass on by.
  The sun will be there
  Even if you can't see it,
  Always be there,
  I can guarantee it.

2 How about you,
  Sometimes?
  Are you lost, too,
  Sometimes?
  Caught up in roundabout schemes?
  Gives this a try
  Sometimes,
  Set your sights high
  Sometimes,
  Simply try changing the scene,
  I'm sure you know what I mean.

  Chorus
  Look in the sky,
  Tell all the clouds to pass on by.
  The sun will be there
  Even if you can't see it,
  Always be there,
  I can guarantee it,
  Every time.

  David Stoll

23

90

1 I come like a beggar with a gift in my hand;
I come like a beggar with a gift in my hand.
By the hungry I will feed you,
By the poor I'll make you rich,
By the broken I will mend you.
Tell me,
Which one is which?

2 I come like a prisoner to bring you the key,
I come like a prisoner to bring you the key.
By the hungry I will feed you,
By the poor I'll make you rich,
By the broken I will mend you.
Tell me,
Which one is which?

3 The need of another is the gift that I bring,
The need of another is the gift that I bring.
By the hungry I will feed you,
By the poor I'll make you rich,
By the broken I will mend you.
Tell me,
Which one is which?

4 Take the wine that I bring you and the bread
that I break,
Take the wine that I bring you and the bread
that I break.
By the hungry I will feed you,
By the poor I'll make you rich,
By the broken I will mend you.
Tell me,
Which one is which?

Sydney Carter

91

1 You can build a wall around you,
   Stone by stone, a solid ring;
   You can live alone, in an empty home,
   Be in charge and be the king.

   Chorus:
   Break out, reach out,
   Make the walls crumble down, down, down.
   Break out, reach out,
   Make the walls tumble down.

2 You can build a wall around you,
   Stop the sun from shining in;
   There'll be snow-topped trees and a chilling
   breeze,
   Always winter, never spring.
   Chorus

3 You can build a wall around you,
   Slam the door shut fast and firm;
   There's no friend at hand who can understand,
   To love you, and help you learn.
   Chorus

                              Geoffrey Gardner

This is based on Oscar Wilde's story 'The selfish giant'.

92

1 When night arrives and chills the skies,
   And stillness settles across the land,
   The hazy moon shines in the gloom
   And shadows shudder close at hand.

   Chorus
   Sing, sing, our praises bring,
   The dawn lights up the distant east,
   Sing, sing our praises bring,
   The sun will come in its glory.

2 No sound is heard from sleeping birds,
And frost is white on the roads and grass;
There are no signs of warmer times,
No buds to show that winter's passed.
Chorus

3 When darkest fears and thoughts appear,
The clouds are grey and cheerless,
When friends have gone, we're all alone,
The day looks cold and lifeless.
Chorus

Geoffrey Gardner

93

1 Morning sun, morning sun,
Lights the day that's just begun,
Helping everyone to see
How beautiful the world can be.

2 Midday sun, midday sun,
All the warmest light has come,
Brightening our lives below,
Helping all the plants to grow.

3 Setting sun, setting sun,
When the day is nearly done,
Moving all the light away,
Till you rise another day.

4 Shining sun, shining sun,
Bringing life to everyone,
Helping all the world to see,
You shine on us eternally.

Jill Darby

94

1 (1) Make us worthy, Lord,
  (2) *Make us worthy, Lord.*
  (1) To serve our fellow men,
  (2) *To serve our fellow men.*
  (1) Make us worthy, Lord,
  (2) *Make us worthy, Lord.*
  (1) To serve our fellow men,
  (2) *To serve our fellow men.*
  (1) Throughout the world who live and die,
  (2) *Throughout the world who live and die,*
  (1) In poverty and hunger,
  (2) *In poverty and hunger,*
  (1) In poverty and hunger,
  (2) *In poverty and hunger.*

2 (1) Give them, through our hands,
  (2) *Give them, through our hands,*
  (1) This day, their daily bread,
  (2) *This day, their daily bread.*
  (1) Give them, through our hands,
  (2) *Give them, through our hands,*
  (1) This day, their daily bread,
  (2) *This day, their daily bread.*
  (1) And by our understanding love,
  (2) *And by our understanding love,*
  (1) Give peace and joy,
  (2) *Give peace and joy,*
  (1) Give peace and joy,
  (2) *Give peace and joy.*

Traditional

*This is often known as 'Mother Teresa's Daily
Prayer'. The song can be sung by two groups,
indicated by (1) and (2). Group (2) echoes the
tune and words sung by Group (1). Alternatively,
it may be sung without the echoing phrases.*

Short version

1 Make us worthy, Lord,
  To serve our fellow men;
  Make us worthy, Lord,
  To serve our fellow men,

Throughout the world who live and die,
In poverty and hunger,
In poverty and hunger.

2 Give them, through our hands,
This day, their daily bread;
Give them, through our hands,
This day, their daily bread,
And by our understanding love,
Give peace and joy,
Give peace and joy.

95

Rejoice in the Lord always
and again I say rejoice.
Rejoice in the Lord always
and again I say rejoice.
Rejoice, rejoice,
and again I say rejoice,
Rejoice, rejoice,
and again I say rejoice.

Traditional

This is based on Philippians 4:4. The song may be sung as a round.

96

1 A still small voice in the heart of the city,
A still small voice on the mountain,
Through the storms that are raging or the quiet
of the evening,
It can only be heard if you listen.

2 The voice of God in a place that is troubled,
The voice of God in the dawn,
Through the noise of the shouting,
Through the still sound of the sleeping,
It can only be heard if you listen.

3 Give time to hear, give us love to listen,
Give wisdom for understanding,
There's a still, small voice which to each one is
speaking,
If we only have the time to listen.

Jancis Harvey

97 'Tis the gift to be simple, 'tis the gift to be free,
'Tis the gift to come down where you ought to be,
And when we find ourselves in the place just right,
'Twill be in the valley of love and delight.

Chorus:
When true simplicity is gained,
To bow and to bend we shan't be ashamed;
To turn, turn will be our delight,
Till by turning, turning we come round right.

Traditional. A Shaker song. The melody of 'Lord of the Dance' is based on this tune.

98 You shall go out with joy and be led forth with peace,
And the mountains and the hills shall break forth before you,
There'll be shouts of joy and the trees of the fields
Shall clap, shall clap their hands.
And the trees of the field shall clap their hands,
And the trees of the field shall clap their hands,
And the trees of the field shall clap their hands,
And you'll go out with joy.
                Stuart Dauermann and Steffi Geiser Rubin

This is based on the words of Isaiah 55:12. The song can be repeated, getting faster each time.

99

Chorus:
Love will never come to an end,
Love will never come to an end,
Three things will last:
Faith, hope and love,
But greatest of all is love,
Love, love, love.

1 Like an angel I may speak,
   Know the truths that others seek,
   Give my goods and life away,
   I am nothing without love.
   Chorus

2 I may seem a great success,
   Wisdom, wealth or charm possess,
   Yet whatever I achieve
   I am nothing without love.
   Chorus

3 Love is patient, love is kind.
   Love requires a truthful mind.
   Love will keep no score of wrongs.
   There is nothing love can't face.
   Chorus

4 Childish thoughts are put away,
   Partial knowledge has its day.
   Love with faith and hope endures,
   There is nothing conquers love.

Chorus:
Love will never come to an end,
Love will never come to an end,
Three things will last:
Faith, hope and love,
But greatest of all is love,
Love, love, love.
Love is forever,
For ever and ever, is love.

Patrick Appleford

This is based on words from 1 Corinthians 13.

100

1 I may speak in the tongues of angels
　And foretell with a heavenly song;
　Should it be that my love is lacking —
　Then my voice is a sounding gong;

　Chorus:
　Three things last for ever,
　They are faith, hope and love;
　And the greatest of these is love,
　And the greatest of these is love!

2 I may give all I have to neighbours,
　And explore every mansion above
　To possess all the jewels of wisdom —
　I am nothing at all, without love;
　Chorus

3 By my faith I may move the mountains,
　And may stand for a cause to be won;
　If I do not have love in doing —
　Then I shall be the better by none;
　Chorus

4 Now this loving is kind and generous,
　And a wonderful, glorious sign
　Of the limitless, deep, compassion
　From the Power, supremely divine;
　Chorus

　　　　　　　　　　　　　Ronald Green

This is based on words from 1 Corinthians 13.

101

1 In the bustle of the city,
　There is life, there is love;
　In the birdsong of the country,
　There is life, there is love;
　Down the streets and down the lanes,
　Through the wind and through the flames,
　Where the human heart is beating,
　Give your life, give your love.

2 Where the voices lift in laughter,
There is life, there is love;
Where the tears fall from the crying,
There is life, there is love;
During health and during pain,
Through the sunshine, through the rain,
Where the human heart is beating,
Give your life, give your love.

3 See the families, see the lonely,
There is life, there is love;
With the sheltered, with the homeless,
There is life, there is love;
To the young and to the old,
Through the warm and through the cold,
Where the human heart is beating,
Give your life, give your love.

4 In the factory and garden,
There is life, there is love,
For the worker and the jobless,
There is life, there is love;
To all men and to all women,
Through their dying and their living,
Where the human heart is beating,
Give your life, give your love.

Geoffrey Gardner

102

1 You can't stop rain from falling down,
Prevent the sun from shining,
You can't stop spring from coming in,
Or winter from resigning,
Or still the waves or stay the winds,
Or keep the day from dawning;
You can't stop God from loving you,
His love is new each morning.

2 You can't stop ice from being cold,
You can't stop fire from burning,
Or hold the tide that's going out,
Delay its sure returning,

32

Or halt the progress of the years,
The flight of fame and fashion;
You can't stop God from loving you,
His nature is compassion.

3 You can't stop God from loving you,
Though you may have ignored him,
You can't stop God from loving you,
However you betray him;
From love like this no power on earth
The human heart can sever,
You can't stop God from loving you,
Not God, not now, nor ever.

John Gowans

103

Chorus:
I am planting my feet in the footsteps
That are there before me everyday.
Taking my journey one step at a time
The footsteps will guide me all the way.

1 The road of life lies before me,
And I know that's the way I must tread.
But I have the signs there to guide me,
And my path before is clear ahead.
Chorus

2 There arc turnings that sometimes look
brighter,
And ways that seem better to me.
And people who'd stop me from travelling,
But I'll keep to the footsteps I see.
Chorus

3 It's easy somedays to feel weary,
And tire when the journey is long;
But streams always soothe and refresh me,
And footsteps ahead lead me on.
Chorus

Jancis Harvey

104

1 Time is a thing
Like a bird on the wing,
Coming or going away.
Time is a thing
Like a bird on the wing,
Coming or going away.
Coming or gone,
You're travelling on,
There's nowhere you can stay.
Coming or gone,
You're travelling on,
You're always on the way.

2 Love is a thing
Like a bird on the wing,
Coming or going away.
Love is a thing
Like a bird on the wing,
Coming or going away.
Coming or gone,
You're travelling on,
There's nowhere you can stay.
Coming or gone,
You're travelling on,
You're always on the way.

3 Hope is a thing
Like a bird on the wing,
Coming or going away.
Hope is a thing
Like a bird on the wing,
Coming or going away.
Coming or gone,
You're travelling on,
There's nowhere you can stay.
Coming or gone,
You're travelling on,
You're always on the way.

Sydney Carter

105

1 God of the morning, at whose voice
The cheerful sun makes haste to rise,
And, like a giant, does rejoice
To run his journey through the skies.

Chorus:
On, on, the blazing sun,
Give again your living light,
On, on, till day is done,
Shine again and bring new life.

2 From distant places of the east
The circuit of his race begins,
And, without weariness or rest,
Around the world he flies and shines.
Chorus

3 Just like the sun, may we complete
The tasks we have to do this day,
With ready mind and active will
Move on, with hope along our way.
Chorus

Isaac Watts, with extra words by Geoffrey Gardner

106

1 It's a new day, there's hope,
It's a new day, there's scope,
To face a different challenge,
Discover that there's no end
To new beginnings
To the new things we can do.

2 It's a new task, there's hope,
It's a new task, there's scope,
To face a different challenge,
Discover that there's no end
To new beginnings,
To the new things we can do.

3 It's a new skill, there's hope,
It's a new skill, there's scope . . .

4 It's a new friend, there's hope,
It's a new friend, there's scope . . .

5 It's a new year, there's hope,
It's a new year, there's scope . . .

6 It's a new week, there's hope,
It's a new week, there's scope . . .

Geoffrey Gardner
Choose the verses most appropriate for your needs.

107

1 You've got to move when the spirit says move,
You've got to move when the spirit says move,
'Cos when the spirit says move,
You've got to move when the spirit,
Move when the spirit says move.

2 You've got to sing when the spirit says sing,
You've got to sing when the spirit says sing,
'Cos when the spirit says sing,
You've got to sing when the spirit,
Sing when the spirit says sing.

3 You've got to clap when the spirit says clap,
You've got to clap when the spirit says clap,
'Cos when the spirit says clap,
You've got to clap when the spirit,
Clap when the spirit says clap.

4 You've got to shout when the spirit says shout,
You've got to shout when the spirit says shout,
'Cos when the spirit says shout,
You've got to shout when the spirit,
Shout when the spirit says shout.

5 You've got to move when the spirit says move,
You've got to move when the spirit says move,
'Cos when the spirit says move,
You've got to move when the spirit,
Move when the spirit says move.

Traditional

108

1 The Lord, the Lord, the Lord is my shepherd.
The Lord, the Lord, the Lord is my shepherd.
The Lord, the Lord, the Lord is my shepherd.
The Lord is my shepherd and I shall not want.

2 He makes me lie down in green, green
pastures.
He makes me lie down in green, green
pastures.
He makes me lie down in green, green
pastures.
The Lord is my shepherd and I shall not want.

3 He leads me beside the still, still waters.
He leads me beside the still, still waters.
He leads me beside the still, still waters.
The Lord is my shepherd and I shall not want.

Traditional, based on Psalm 23

109

1 Thank you for the summer morning
misting into heat;
Thank you for the diamonds
of dew beneath my feet;
Thank you for the silver
where a snail has wandered by;
Oh, we praise the name
of him who made
the earth and sea and sky.

2 Thank you for the yellow fields
of corn like waving hair;
Thank you for the red surprise
of poppies here and there;
Thank you for the blue of
an electric dragon-fly;
Oh, we praise the name
of him who made
the earth and sea and sky.

3 Thank you for the splintered light
among the brooding trees;
Thank you for the leaves that rustle
in a sudden breeze;
Thank you for the branches
and the fun of climbing high;
Oh, we praise the name
of him who made
the earth and sea and sky.

4 Thank you for the evening
as the light begins to fade,
Clouds so red and purple
that the setting sun has made;
Thank you for the shadows
as the owls come gliding by;
Oh, we praise the name
of him who made
the earth and sea and sky.

Susan Sayers

110

1 Sing, people, sing,
  And follow in a ring,
  Praise to God for all we do,
  Marching, seeing, hearing, too;
  Sing, people, sing,
  Sing, people, sing.

2 March, come on, march,
  Beneath the springtime arch;
  Primroses a special sight,
  Cowslips make the garden bright,
  March, come on, march,
  March, come on, march.

3 March, come on, march,
  Beneath the summer arch;
  Roses in the hedges high,
  Honeysuckle climbing by,
  March, come on, march,
  March, come on, march,

4 March, come on, march,
  Beneath the autumn arch;
  Hazel nuts are turning brown,
  Chestnuts too are falling down;
  March, come on, march,
  March, come on, march.

5 Sing, people, sing,
  And follow in a ring,
  Praise to God for all we do,
  Marching, seeing, hearing, too;
  Sing, people, sing,
  Sing, people, sing.

Traditional

///

Chorus:
Round, round, round go the seasons,
Turn, turn, turn goes the time,
On, on, on go the days and nights.
The circle's a changing sign,
The circle's a changing sign.

1 Swallows nesting on the wall,
Swoop in the summer air,
Fly a thousand miles to warmer skies,
There will be more next year, we hope,
There will be more next year.
Chorus

2 Sticky buds on chestnut trees,
Burst into candle flowers,
Bronze and glistening conkers hit the ground,
There will be more next year, we hope,
There will be more next year.
Chorus

3 Toads and frogs make for their ponds,
Swim and lay their spawn.
Twist and wriggle worm-like, changing shape
There will be more next year, we hope,
There will be more next year.
Chorus

Geoffrey Gardner

112

1 Lay my white cloak on the ground,
  Spring isn't coming, spring isn't coming;
  Cold, cold snow falling all around,
  Spring isn't coming this year.
  Paint the trees with my silver frost,
  Spring isn't coming, spring isn't coming;
  Under ice the earth is lost,
  Spring isn't coming this year.

2 My cold wind will make you frown,
  Spring isn't coming, spring isn't coming;
  Blow the chimney pots all down!
  Spring isn't coming this year.
  Breath of ice and cloak of grey,
  Spring isn't coming, spring isn't coming;
  Rattle hailstones all the day,
  Spring isn't coming this year.

3 Hear sweet birdsong fill the air,
  Spring will be coming, spring will be coming;
  Sunshine smiling everywhere,
  Spring will be coming once more.
  Through the soil the flowers peep,
  Spring will be coming, spring will be coming;
  Earth is waking from her sleep,
  Spring will be coming once more.
                    Alison J. Carver

This is based on Oscar Wilde's story 'The selfish giant'.

113

Chorus:
To ev'rything, turn, turn, turn,
There is a season, turn, turn, turn,
And a time for ev'ry purpose under heaven.

1 A time to be born, a time to die;
  A time to plant, a time to reap;
  A time to kill, a time to heal;
  A time to laugh, a time to weep.
  Chorus

41

2 A time to build up, a time to break down;
A time to dance, a time to mourn;
A time of love, a time of hate;
A time of war, a time of peace.
Chorus

3 A time to lose, a time to gain;
A time to tear, a time to mend;
A time to love, a time to hate;
A time for peace, I swear it's not too late.
Chorus

Pete Seeger

This is based on the words of Ecclesiastes 3.

114

Chorus:
Flickering candles in the night;
Darkness turning into light.
Flickering candles in the night;
Darkness turning into light.

1 Gather round the winter fire,
Stop the chill wind's blow;
Watch the flame and feel the warmth,
Hands and faces glow.
Chorus

2 Cards and streamers on the walls,
Brighten up the room;
Decorations, coloured lamps,
Drive away the gloom.
Chorus

3 Tell a story from the past;
Celebrate in song;
Those who changed despair to hope,
And defeated wrong.
Chorus

Geoffrey Gardner

Suitable for Christmas, Hannukah and Diwali.

115

1 'Come in, my royal masters,
I'm glad to have you stay.
I welcome you, and ask you
A question, if I may?
Why have you come this distance
From where your kingdoms are?
Oh, tell me, noble sirs, why are you journeying
so far?'

'Baboushka, oh, Baboushka, we're following a
star,
Baboushka, oh, Baboushka, we're following a
star.'

2 'The star's a mighty marvel,
A truly glorious sight.
But, lords, you must stay longer —
Oh, won't you stay the night?
Do tell me why you hurry —
And here's another thing:
I marvel at the meaning of the precious gifts
you bring.'

'Baboushka, oh, Baboushka, they're for a new-
born king.
Baboushka, oh, Baboushka, they're for a new-
born king.'

3 'Some king, to have such treasure,
A star to show his birth,
And you to do him honour,
The greatest ones of earth —
And yet he is a baby,
A tiny man is he?
O royal ones, I wonder, then, if he will
welcome me?'

'Baboushka, oh, Baboushka, oh, why not
come and see?
Baboushka, oh, Baboushka, oh, why not come
and see?'

Continued overleaf

4 'I will, my royal masters —
But not just now, I fear.
I'll follow on tomorrow
When I have finished here.
My home I must make tidy,
And sweep and polish, too,
And then some gifts I must prepare — I have
so much to do!'

'Baboushka, oh, Baboushka, we dare not wait
for you.
Baboushka, oh, Baboushka, we dare not wait
for you.'

5 At last I make the journey —
No star to lead me on.
Good people, can you tell me
The way the kings have gone?
Some shepherds tell of angels
But now there is no sound.
The stable, it is empty, and the baby Egypt-
bound.

'Baboushka, oh, Baboushka, we know where
he is found.
Baboushka, oh, Baboushka, we know where
he is found.'

6 Through all the years I seek him
I feel him very near
O people, do you know him?
Oh, tell me: Is he here?
In all the world I travel
But late I made my start.
Oh, tell me if you find him for I've searched in
every part.

'Baboushka, oh, Baboushka, we find him in
our heart.
Baboushka, oh, Baboushka, we find him in our
heart.'

Arthur Scholey

*This is based on the Russian story of Baboushka,
an old lady who, because she was too busy, mis-
sed the Christ Child in Bethlehem.*

116

1 There's a star in the east on Christmas morn,
Rise up, shepherd, and follow;
It'll lead to the place where the Saviour's born,
Rise up, shepherd, and follow.
   Leave your sheep, and leave your lambs,
   Rise up, shepherd, and follow,
   Leave your ewes and leave your rams,
   Rise up, shepherd, and follow.
   Follow, follow,
   Rise up, shepherd, and follow,
   Follow the star of Bethlehem,
   Rise up, shepherd, and follow.

2 If you take good heed to the angel's words,
Rise up, shephered, and follow,
You'll forget your flocks and forget your herds,
Rise up, shepherd, and follow.
   Leave your sheep, and leave your lambs,
   Rise up, shepherd, and follow,
   Leave your ewes and leave your rams,
   Rise up, shepherd, and follow.
   Follow, follow,
   Rise up, shepherd, and follow,
   Follow the star of Bethlehem,
   Rise up, shepherd, and follow.

Traditional

117

1 I want to see your baby boy,
But have no gift for you,
So, Mary, if you'll pardon me
There's one thing I can do:

   Chorus:
   I'll sing a song,
   A special song,
   Written for a king;
   I bring a song,
   A special song,
   I bring a song to sing.

2 I've never heard of myrrh before,
I don't know where it's found.
I haven't any frankincense,
There's not much gold around:
Chorus

3 I have no words of good advice
To help him on his way,
But there is one thing I can do
Upon this special day:
Chorus

Elizabeth Bennett

118

1 When the winter day is dying
And the wind is blowing wild,
Listen for a lonely crying,
It may be the wandering Child.
Light a candle in your window
Let the night know that you care.
Light a candle in the window,
It may guide the Christ-Child there.

2 When at times you fear to follow
On the track that you must tread,
Friendly promises are hollow
For the tests that lie ahead —
Light a candle in your window
When your final hope is gone.
Light a candle in the window,
And the Child will lead you on.

3 When the world outside is waiting
But you can't give any more —
There's no end to war and hating
And you long to close the door —
Light a candle in your window
Let it shine beyond your pain.
Light a candle in the window,
And the Child will come again.

Arthur Scholey

119

1 The holly and the ivy,
   When they are both full grown;
   Of all the trees that are in the wood,
   The holly bears the crown:

   Chorus:
   The rising of the sun,
   And the running of the deer,
   The playing of the merry organ,
   Sweet singing in the choir.

2 The holly bears a blossom,
   As white as the lily flower;
   And Mary bore sweet Jesus Christ,
   To be our sweet Saviour:
   Chorus

3 The holly bears a berry,
   As red as any blood;
   And Mary bore sweet Jesus Christ
   To do poor sinners good.
   Chorus

4 The holly bears a prickle,
   As sharp as any thorn,
   And Mary bore sweet Jesus Christ
   On Christmas Day in the morn:
   Chorus

5 The holly bears a bark,
   As bitter as any gall;
   And Mary bore sweet Jesus Christ
   For to redeem us all:
   Chorus

6 The holly and the ivy,
   When they are both full grown,
   Of all the trees that are in the wood,
   The holly bears the crown:
   Chorus

                              Traditional

120

1 As I went riding by,
  I saw a star in the sky;
  I followed where it led —
  And found a manger bed:

  Chorus:
  Little Jesus, show me the way of your love,
  Little Jesus, show me the way of your love.

2 As I stood quietly still,
  Some shepherds came from the hill;
  Their eyes were bright with joy —
  To find the baby boy:
  Chorus

3 As I went riding back,
  Some camels passed on the track;
  Three kings had seen the star —
  And hurried from afar:
  Chorus

4 As I rode home to bed,
  A thought came into my head:
  God must love ev'ryone —
  To give the world his son:
  Chorus

                              Cecily Taylor

121

1 The Virgin Mary had a baby boy,
The Virgin Mary had a baby boy,
The Virgin Mary had a baby boy,
And they say that his name was Jesus.

Chorus:
He came from the glory,
He came from the glorious kingdom;
He came from the glory,
He came from the glorious kingdom.
Oh, yes, believer!
Oh, yes, believer!
He came from glory,
He came from the glorious kingdom.

2 The angels sang when the baby was born,
The angels sang when the baby was born,
The angels sang when the baby was born,
And they say that his name was Jesus.
Chorus

3 The shepherds ran to see the baby boy,
The shepherds ran to see the baby boy,
The shepherds ran to see the baby boy,
And they say that his name was Jesus.
Chorus

4 The wise men wondered where the baby was
born,
The wise men wondered where the baby was
born,
The wise men wondered where the baby was
born,
And they say that his name was Jesus.
Chorus

Traditional

122

Christmas, Christmas, celebrate the time of
year.
Special days and special customs,
Special foods and special gifts.
Raise your voices in a greeting:
'Happy festival!' That's our wish.

Geoffrey Gardner

*This can be used for most popular festivals:
Easter, Diwali, Navratri, Holi, Hannukah, Sukkot, Passover, Eid, Baisakhi, etc. Substitute the
name of the appropriate festival. The song can be
sung several times, possibly becoming faster each
time.*

123

1 Mary had a baby, yes, Lord;
Mary had a baby, yes, my Lord;
Mary had a baby, yes, Lord;
The people came to worship him in
Bethlehem.

2 What did she name him? Yes, Lord . . .

3 She called him Jesus, yes, Lord . . .

4 Where was he born? Yes, Lord . . .

5 Born in a stable, yes, Lord . . .

6 Where did they lay him? Yes, Lord . . .

7 Laid him in a manger, yes, Lord . . .

Traditional

124

1 Riding out across the desert,
Travelling over sandy plains,
Comes a company of wise men,
Moving steadily along their way;
Leaving all their friends behind them,
Guided by the star so bright,
Now they've got to keep on going
Must not let the star get out of sight.

Chorus:
Riding through the desert,
Gently the wise men go,
Onwards to the king,
Who was promised long ago;
But they don't know where they're going to find
him,
There's many towns to search,
So they'll keep on following the star,
For it will lead them to his place of birth.

2 Wise men on their desert journey,
Travelled many miles so far,
Though they're getting tired and weary,
Town of Bethlehem is not too far:
How they long to worship Jesus
And honour him with royal gifts,
Hearts are full of joy and wonder,
As they're searching for the new born king.
Chorus

Peter Ratcliffe

125

Chorus:
Standing in the rain,
Knocking on the window,
Knocking on the window
On a Christmas day.
There he is again,
Knocking on the window,
Knocking on the window
In the same old way.

1 No use knocking on the window,
There is nothing we can do, sir;
All the beds are booked already,
There is nothing left for you, sir!
Chorus

2 No, we haven't got a manger,
No, we haven't got a stable;
Till you woke us with your knocking,
We were sleeping like the dead, sir!
Chorus

Sydney Carter

126

Chorus
Little star stay with us,
Lighten the darkness;
Shine through this long night
And show us the way.

1 Little star shining,
Tonight we are feeling
You leading us home
Though the journey is long.
All down the centuries
Travellers have seen you,
And welcomed the warmth
Of your silent night song.
Chorus

2 Once you gave light
To a dimly lit stable,
And melted the chill,
Where the new baby lay;
Silently, gently,
His sleeping you guarded,
And stayed till the dawn
Of another new day.
Chorus

Jancis Harvey

127

1 Christmas time is here,
Come and celebrate,
Come and celebrate,
Come and celebrate,
Christmas time is here,
Come and celebrate,
Lift your voice in song.

2 Decorate your rooms,
Come and celebrate . . .

3 Gather with your friends,
Come and celebrate . . .

4 Meet to worship God,
Come and celebrate . . .

5 Hear the tales of old,
Come and celebrate . . .

6 Share the special food,
Come and celebrate . . .

7 See the lighted lamps,
Come and celebrate . . .
            Geoffrey Gardner

*'Christmas time is here', could be replaced by the
names of other festivals:*

Hinduism
Diwali is here
Navratri is here
Holi time is here

Judaism
Pesach time is here (*Passover*)
Rosh Hashanah's here (*The New Year*)
Purim time is here
Sukkot time is here
Hannukah is here

Sikhism
Baisakhi is here
The Guru's day is here (*for Guru Nanak's Birthday*)

Christianity
Advent time is here
Easter time is here
Whitsun time is here
Pentecost is here
Harvest time is here

Islam
Eid ul Fitr's here
The Prophet's day is here (*for the Birthday of the Prophet*).

128

1 Trotting, trotting through Jerusalem,
Jesus sitting on a donkey's back,
Children waving branches, singing,
'Happy is he that comes in the name of the Lord!'

2 Many people in Jerusalem
Thought he should have come on a mighty horse,
Lead his nation into battle —
'Happy is he that comes in the name of the Lord!'

3 Many people in Jerusalem
Were amazed to see such a quiet man
Trotting, trotting on a donkey,
'Happy is he that comes in the name of the Lord!'

4 Trotting, trotting through Jerusalem,
Jesus sitting on a donkey's back,
Let us all join in the singing,
'Happy is he that comes in the name of the Lord!'

Eric Reid

129

1 Jesus in the garden,
 Sad and left alone,
 Soldiers come to take him;
 His friends have run for home.
   Jesus in the courtroom,
   Sad and left alone,
   People come to mock him
   In robe and crown of thorns.

2 Jesus on the hillside,
 Sad and left alone,
 In the silent darkness
 He dies there on his own.
   Hiding in their home,
   Disciples lock the door,
   Frightened of the people;
   They go outside no more.

3 Disciples in the room
 Feel sadness turn to joy,
 Know there's work for them to do,
 Throw open wide the door.
   Disciples meet the crowds
   To share their joy with them,
   Dance and sing to tell about
   The man from Nazareth,
   The man from Nazareth,
   The man from Nazareth,
 (Nazareth)

John Tearnan

130

1 All in an Easter garden,
 Before the break of day,
 An angel came for Jesus,
 And rolled the stone away.
 And when his friends came seeking,
 With myrrh and spices rare,
 They found the angels at the door,
 But Jesus was not there.

2 All in an Easter garden,
  Where water lilies bloom,
  The angels gave their message,
  Beside an empty tomb;
  'He is not here, but come and see
  The place where Jesus lay:
  The Lord of life is risen indeed,
  For this is Easter Day.'

Traditional

131

1 Now the green blade rises from the buried
  grain,
  Wheat that in the dark earth many days has
  lain:
  Love lives again, that with the dead has been:
  Love is come again like wheat that's springing
  green.

2 In the grave they laid him, love whom men had
  slain,
  Thinking that never he would wake again:
  Laid in the earth like grain that sleeps unseen:
  Love is come again like wheat that's springing
  green.

3 Forth he came at Easter, like the risen grain,
  He that for three days in the grave had lain:
  Live from the dead my risen Lord is seen:
  Love is come again like wheat that's springing
  green.

4 When our hearts are wintry, grieving or in
  pain,
  Your touch can call us back to life again:
  Fields of our heart that dead and bare have
  been:
  Love is come again like wheat that's springing
  green.

J. M. C. Crum (adapted by Geoffrey Gardner)

132

1 When from the sky, in the splendour of
  summer,
  Sunlight pours down over roof, over wood,
  We sing of the kindness, extravagant kindness,
  Of God who is Father and Lord of all good.

2 When all around us the glory of autumn
  Colours the gardens, the fields and the hills,
  We sing of the wonder, unspeakable wonder,
  Of God who with joy both begins and fulfils.

3 When in the coldness and deadness of winter
  Storms from the east with their bluster begin,
  We sing of that morning, mysterious morning,
  When Jesus was born in the barn of an inn.

4 When in the gladness and greenness of
  springtime
  Winter is over in life and in light,
  We sing of that Easter, miraculous Easter,
  That shattered the darkness and dread of the
  night.

Alan T. Dale

133

Chorus
Lord of the harvest, Lord of the field,
Give thanks now to God in nature revealed.

1 Give thanks for the sun, the wind and the rain
  And thanks for the crops that feed us again.
  The corn safely cut is gathered inside
  We thank you, oh Lord, that you can provide.
  Chorus

2 The trees ripe with fruit stand proud in the sun,
  We gather them now that summer is gone.
  For yours is the wonder, yours is the power,
  Yours is the glory of fruit and of flower.
  Chorus

3 So in all our plenty, help us to see,
The needs all around whatever they be.
With food for the body, strength for the soul,
It's healing and caring, making them whole.
Chorus

Jancis Harvey

134

1 I planted a seed
And now that seed is growing,
Oh, how that seed is growing
Out of all the ground of me!
I planted a seed,
But there's no way of knowing,
But there's no way of knowing,
Is it fruit or flower or weed?
There is no way of showing
'Till it blooms for all to see.

2 I planted a thought
And now that thought is taking,
Oh, how that thought is taking
Over all the mind of me!
I planted a thought,
And, love or hate, it's breaking,
And, love or hate, it's breaking
Out and never will be caught;
And love or hate it's making
Of the way you think of me.

3 I planted a word
And now that word is yelling,
Oh, how that word is yelling
Out of all the mouth of me!
I planted a word
And truth or lie it's telling,
And truth or lie it's telling
Just whenever it is heard.
Whatever it is spelling,
It will soon be clear to see.

4 I planted a deed
   And now that deed is spreading,
   Oh, how that deed is spreading
   Far beyond the reach of me!
   I planted a deed,
   For good or bad it's heading,
   For good or bad it's heading —
   Oh who knows where it will lead?
   Should I be glad, or dreading —
   Here it comes straight back to me!

Arthur Scholey

135

1 Pears and apples, wheat and grapes,
   Many textures, many shapes;
   Falling leaves in golden drifts
   Thank you, God, for harvest gifts.

2 Flashing shoals of silver fish,
   Every colour you could wish;
   Fishing boats, for you and me
   Reap the harvest of the sea.

3 Deep beneath the ocean floor
   Fuel and power have lain in store,
   Brought to us through dangerous toil
   Thank you, God, for gas and oil.

4 Coal black diamonds in the earth,
   Ancient forests gave them birth;
   Skill and labour now combine
   Reaping harvests of the mine.

5 Earth and ocean, plant and beast,
   Altogether make the feast;
   All who long to share your grace
   At your table have their place.

6 Loving Lord, we know you care;
   May we all your goodness share;
   Save us from all selfish greed,
   Finding you in those in need.

Paul Booth

136

1 We thank you, Lord, for all we eat,
   From farmers' fields and oceans deep;
   We thank you too for those who toil
   The long year round on sea and soil.

2 In stormy seas and shrieking gales,
   In snow and ice and thunderous hail,
   Men plough the waves and sow their nets;
   They reap their harvest cold and wet.

3 From break of day till darkness falls,
   In summer sun and winter squalls,
   Our land is worked and tilled and sown,
   'Till all hands ache and all backs groan.

4 We thank you too for those who drive
   To bring our food where we can buy.
   In shops and stores and market square,
   So many work to help us there.

5 For those who live in distant lands
   And work so hard in dust and sand;
   Dear Lord, we pray that they will too
   Have food enough to eat and grow.

Robert Smith

137

1 Michaelmas daisies purple in the border,
   Big fat leeks all standing up in order,
   Whiskered barley talking to the breeze,
   Low hung boughs of laden apple trees,
   Chugging engines ready for the reaping,
   Pounds of chutney labelled for the keeping,
   Giant marrows winning every prize,
   Bubbling jars of elderberry wine;
   It's harvest time, harvest time again,
   Harvest time, thanks to sun and rain,
   A time to take and a time to give,
   A time to say that it's a joy to live.

2 Stocky-built trawlers landing with their
     catches,
   Berries gathered, never mind the scratches,
   Warm and hazy Indian summer days,
   Swallows leaving for another place,
   Fruits are bottled, others in the deep freeze,
   Silken poppies blushing in the corn-fields,
   'Don't bring muddy boots into the hall!',
   Golden onions hanging on a wall;
   It's harvest time, harvest time again,
   Harvest time, thanks to sun and rain,
   A time to take and a time to give,
   A time to say that it's a joy to live
   At harvest time.
   Mellow, fruitful harvest time.

Estelle White

138

1 Now we sing a harvest song,
   Clear and joyful, loud and strong,
   Think of bread and think of meat,
   Think of all we have to eat,
   All God's gifts to us in love,
   Earth and rain and sun above,
   Thank you, God, for all you give,
   Thank you, God, by whom we live.

2 Now we sing a sadder song,
   Of injustice, hunger, wrong,
   Those with not enough to eat,
   Suffering every sort of need.
   They've no home, no work, no pay.
   Scraping through from day to day.
   Do they thank you that they live?
   Thank you, God, that we can give.

3 As we sing our harvest song,
   Clear and joyful, loud and strong,
   Help us, Father, now to see.
   How to set those people free;
   How to share the gifts you give
   So that they may also live,
   So the harvest song may sound
   To your praise the earth around.

Alex Mitchell

139

1 Now the harvest is all gathered,
Let us eat the Sharing Bread;
'In our family, all together,
As our custom is,' we said.
And we pass the Bread among us,
Thanking God that all are fed.

2 But there comes a gentle knocking,
Just before we break the Bread,
From our neighbours in the doorway:
'Harvest failed for us,' they said.
So we share the Bread among them,
Thanking God that all are fed.

3 Soon we hear a growing murmur,
As we eat the Sharing Bread,
From the neighbours of our neighbours:
'We are starving, friends,' it said.
Then we stretch the Bread out further
Thanking God that all are fed.

4 When the world begins to clamour,
We cry, 'Take our Sharing Bread,
Miracles we cannot offer!'
'Oh, it happened once,' they said,
'Thousands of us ate together
Thanking God that all are fed.'

Arthur Scholey

140

(1) Lead me from death to life
(2) *Lead me from death to life,*
(1) From falsehood to truth.
(2) *From falsehood to truth.*

(1) Lead me from despair to hope
(2) *Lead me from despair to hope,*
(1) From fear to trust
(2) *From fear to trust.*

(1) Lead me from hate to love
(2) *Lead me from hate to love,*
(1) From war to peace
(2) *From war to peace.*

(1) Let peace fill our heart, our world
(2) *Let peace fill our heart, our world*
(1) Our universe
(2) *Our universe.*

Short version
Lead me from death to life,
From falsehood to truth.

Lead me from despair to hope,
From fear to trust.

Lead me from hate to love,
From war to peace.

Let peace fill our heart, our world
Our universe.

Adapted by Satish Kumar from 'The Upanishads'. In 1981 Mother Teresa urged everyone to use The Peace Prayer daily. The song can be sung by two groups, indicated by (1) and (2). Group (2) echoes the tune and words sung by Group (1).

141 Shalom, Shalom,
May peace be with you,
Throughout your days;
In all that you do,
May peace be with you,
Shalom, Shalom.
　　　　　Traditional, adapted by Geoffrey Gardner

'Shalom' is a Hebrew word meaning 'peace'. This song may be sung as a round.

142

1 I'm gonna lay down my sword and shield,
Down by the riverside,
Down by the riverside,
Down by the riverside,
I'm gonna lay down my sword and shield,
Down by the riverside,
Down by the riverside.

Chorus:
I ain't gonna study war no more,
I ain't gonna study war no more,
I ain't gonna study war no more;
I ain't gonna study war no more,
I ain't gonna study war no more,
I ain't gonna study war no more,

2 I'm gonna talk with the Prince of peace,
Down by the riverside,
Down by the riverside,
Down by the riverside,
I'm gonna talk with the Prince of peace,
Down by the riverside,
Down by the riverside.
Chorus

3 I'm gonna shake hands with everyone,
Down by the riverside,
Down by the riverside,
Down by the riverside,
I'm gonna shake hands with everyone,
Down by the riverside,
Down by the riverside.
Chorus

4 I'm gonna walk with my friends in peace,
Down by the riverside,
Down by the riverside,
Down by the riverside,
I'm gonna walk with my friends in peace,
Down by the riverside,
Down by the riverside.
Chorus

Traditional

143

1 I've got peace like a river,
Peace like a river,
I've got peace like a river in my soul;
I've got peace like a river,
Peace like a river,
I've got peace like a river in my soul.

2 I've got love like a river,
Love like a river,
I've got love like a river in my soul;
I've got love like a river,
Love like a river,
I've got love like a river in my soul.

3 I've got joy like a river,
Joy like a river,
I've got joy like a river in my soul;
I've got joy like a river,
Joy like a river,
I've got joy like a river in my soul.

4 I've got hope like a river,
Hope like a river,
I've got hope like a river in my soul;
I've got hope like a river,
Hope like a river,
I've got hope like a river in my soul.

Traditional

144

1 Peace is flowing like a river,
Flowing out through you and me,
Spreading out into the desert,
Setting all the people free.

2 Love is flowing like a river,
Flowing out through you and me,
Spreading out into the desert,
Setting all the people free.

3 Joy is flowing like a river,
Flowing out through you and me,
Spreading out into the desert,
Setting all the people free.

4 Hope is flowing like a river,
Flowing out through you and me,
Spreading out into the desert,
Setting all the people free.

Traditional

145

Chorus:
O let us spread the pollen of peace throughout the land;
Let us spread the pollen of peace throughout the land.
Let us spread the pollen of peace, and make all conflict cease,
Let us spread the pollen of peace throughout the land.

1 Jesus has sown the seeds of love;
Jesus has launched the grey winged dove.
Let us make the flower grow,
And let the people know.
That Jesus has sown the seeds of love.
Chorus

2 All it needs is our love to make it grow;
All it needs is our hopefulness to show;
And tell those who are choked with fear
That the prince of peace is here;
All it needs is our love to make it grow.
Chorus

Roger Courtney

This was written by Roger Courtney for the Corrymeela Community, which works to bring peace and reconciliation in Northern Ireland.

146

1 We ask that we live and we labour in peace, in
  peace;
  Each one shall be our neighbour in peace, in
  peace;
  Distrust and hatred will turn to love,
  All the prisoners freed,
  And our only war will be the one
  Against all human need.

2 We work for the end of disunion in truth, in
  truth;
  That all may be one communion in truth, in
  truth;
  We choose the road of peace and prayer
  Countless pilgrims trod,
  So that Hindu, Muslim, Christian, Jew,
  We all can worship one God.

3 We call to our friends and our brothers, unite,
  unite!
  That all may live for others, unite, unite!
  And so the nations will be as one,
  One the flag unfurled,
  One law, one faith, one hope, one truth,
  One people and one world.

Donald Swann

147

1 Make me a channel of your peace.
  Where there is hatred, let me bring your love;
  Where there is injury, your pardon, Lord;
  And where there's doubt, true faith in you:

  Chorus:
  O, Master, grant that I may never seek
  So much to be consoled as to console;
  To be understood as to understand;
  To be loved, as to love with all my soul.

2 Make me a channel of your peace.
  Where there's despair in life, let me bring
  hope;
  Where there is darkness, only light;
  And where there's sadness, ever joy:
  Chorus

3 Make me a channel of your peace.
  It is in pardoning that we are pardoned,
  In giving to all men that we receive,
  And in dying that we're born to eternal life.

Sebastian Temple

This is based on 'The Prayer of St Francis'.

148

Let the world rejoice together, alleluia;
East and west, with north and south sing
alleluia.
Let the world rejoice together, alleluia;
East and west, with north and south sing
alleluia,
Lift your voices, all you people,
Share with others what you can,
Bringing care to those who need it,
Peace in every land,
Peace in every land.
Let the world rejoice together, alleluia,
East and west, with north and south sing
alleluia,
Let the world rejoice together,
alleluia,
East and west, with north and south sing
alleluia.

Geoffrey Gardner
The verse is repeated, getting faster each time.

149

And ev'ryone beneath the vine and the fig tree
Shall live in peace and have no fear (*twice*)
And into plough-shares turn their swords,
Nations shall learn war no more (*twice*)
And ev'ryone beneath the vine and the fig tree
Shall live in peace and have no fear (*twice*)

Traditional

This is based on words from Micah 4:3. This song
may be sung as a round.

INDEX: Page numbers (feint) and song numbers (**bold**)
Titles which are different from the first line
appear in italics.